rose-water syrup

colonized

daughter | muslim | immigrant | feminist | lover

occupied

a poetry collection

Maha Zimmo

ISBN: 978-93-89074-15-4

First Edition: 2019
Rs. 200/-

Cyberwit.net
HIG 45 Kaushambi Kunj, Kalindipuram
Allahabad - 211011 (U.P.) India
http://www.cyberwit.net
Tel: +(91) 9415091004 +(91) (532) 2552257
E-mail: info@cyberwit.net

Printed at Repro India Limited.

for
my mother and aunts,
because of
every woman
of colour
who reminds me that
there is rose-water syrup in our hearts
and steel in our backs.

i cast a net,
catch your rose-water stars
and write structure
to keep the hearts
of my ancestors.

-gratitude | offering

as companion
to her zaatar sandwiches
raining olive oil –

daily,
my grandmother
cried rose-water tears
into her soil
growing cucumbers
plucked
and offered her daughter
as sustenance
for the long walk
to Canada.

it is why
rose-water seeds of home
root
and spring
in my mother's belly.

-an immigrant's mother's intention

i see brown brothers
break open their rib cages
to drink the urine of pale women.
not-my-colour women.
calling it sweet
sweet
mm-mmm
sweet honey.

these same brothers
who close their backs on the rose-water syrup
dripping thick from the hands of my land,
my-skin honey-molasses,
turning noses over yellowed mouths
ever looking for that paler woman.

-the colonized i

he would pick the fullest one from his tree,
lift
and place me
next to him
equal
so i could watch as he unfolded the pomegranate
placing every seed
gently
into rose-water & melted sugar.

i would reach
push into those soft cushions,
rose-water hands,
wait as they slowly refilled
ignoring his task
making a simple unfolding
into an hours-long conversation.

a sea of devotion. principle
were my grandfather's gifts to me.

he
whose pomegranate roots stood long before
Occupation was bre(a)d (& butter)
whose heart direction facing east
still today, especially today
is cause for imprisonment. bullets. bombs.

when he left, and i had to unfold the pomegranate myself,
they told me that

Once upon a time
he had been taken for nine months
a political prisoner
who when returned

first took the hands of my grandmother
and then kissed his children
ate and had his coffee
ended his night
with a small broom
to sweep the carpet of pomegranate
rotten
without his rose-water hands.

-the conversation we never had

while rose-water brothers
have been kneaded with the belief that we are less,
and honey-molasses sisters
with the belief that we are un-whole without our brothers,
i have watched Whitemen
wet at the eyes
drown in the hips of these beautiful sisters
almond eyes
nails dipped in blood.

these same sisters
who have shut their hearts to the rose-water brothers
because
it is easier to choose exoticization over subjugation
when you are taught
that alone
is never enough.

-the colonized ii

in his bookstore
found
distributed by the Occupation, with intention
a qur'an
inside –
one misplaced accent.

gasoline & match
tower in his yard
my grandfather stood
to protect the sanctity of
His word.

-one of the reasons he would become a political prisoner | the night Gaza was ablaze

the last time i saw my grandfather
he gifted me a rose,
delicate mouth
she sang autumn leaves.

when he left for Him
my hands ripped her mouth
burned her tongue
broke her song
fragments next to my heart
laid too on the marble.

after the breaking
i stitched my heart together
and now
kiss my prayers through rose-water tears
lay them among the autumn leaves
a prayer in a prayer that they reach him,
Him.

-jewelry box, in the shape of a rose

my tongue
will remain a switchblade.

a reminder that
you should not
expect
that one of my eyes
turns blind.

-i am not here for your ignorance. racism. sexism. bigotry.
prejudice | in which your discomfort is rooted

People of Colour
who wear brownface
to play people of colour
to the comfort of (those who define us as) Other.

may your History-Rich Depth and Wild Beauty
claw your hands and bare her teeth
every time you reach for that make-up brush.

-a prayer for Us

Whitemen eat fire
for the blush of eyelashes contouring
kohl'd eyes
charcoal hair
kissing hips teardrop-shaped sweeping music
until
our full mouths
speak the language of our ancestors.

Whitemen
ready with ropes
standing before trees
to bind
their terms
hang
what is not.

-sisters, eyes wide shut

we burn the kink straight
peroxide hair
confuse pale skin with (en)light(enment).

we swap blood for alcohol
crisp bacon
face west.

we have learned
to dust our brows with powder instead of soil.

fading our ancestors
because this is the colour of civilzed.

-the colonized iii

she told me of happiness,
a story begun. lived
before Occupation.

when she passed
i found its photograph
(the only photo in her nightstand) -

my grandmother
a child in head-to-toe white
blonde hair halo over
yellow almonds, middle eastern eyes
defiant. strong. proud
square-facing the camera
her Arabian horse to her right
her movement,
freedom,
the one she named: Happiness.

-checkpoint(s) | clairvoyant | what's in a horse's name

i –
see only fire and soil
for bedding
wonder why one would
willfully
with their own hands and by their own choice
choose
to build as home
a (refugee) camp, marshmallows to soften.

i –
want to know.

I.
Want. To. Know.

if this love of camping
if this mirage of Camp
is the reason so many
reduce. erase. nullify
the violence of refugee camps,
self-soothing their hate of Other.

-when they sang campfire songs but i only saw ghosts

i was born
in a country
they have raped
for her oceans of oil.

i am rooted
in a country
without a home country-less
they have suffocated
because of a promise made by Whitemen
to other white men (whom are not viewed as Whitemen by the former).

i call home
a country
whose Whitemen continue to commit the same crimes
against the Indigenous population
as is done against my roots.

and you
you are still surprised by the violence in my mouth.

-intifada

numbers –

the oppressed
the darker skinned
the impoverished
add up

but they
still
call us
'minority'.

-transatlantic | a White narrative of control. domination | they can't sell us what we ain't buyin'

the sun, oracle
wakes daily –

weary
she pushes aside leaves
makes her way down broken streets
past Occupation-dirt windows
smoke. oil. fingerprints covered
hoping she is wrong this day.

her smile mixes with salt-water
as she lights a halo around the faces of Palestinian children
and sees they are
still( )born
with a rope
around their necks.

not today, she thinks
as she retreats
to hope
for a better tomorrow.

-mother(land) | genocide

the voice for whom we speak
is s/he whose body is pinned to the ground
with a boot on their neck.

you are free
to close your chest
to the pain of others

apathy, it is your right.
(Apathy, it is your *right*?)

but
when you stitch your lips to one another
your hands are not softened by neutrality
the thread not without violence.

it remains you
actively
sending your hands up from the ground
behind these bodies
wrapping themselves around the boot
and slowly pulling down
toward yourself
where you lie in the dirt.

-before you next wear your stupidity on your mouth | 'i don't get involved in politics'

fear
is the path between knowing what is right
and where you stand today.

courage
is the crossing of this path.

it is the folding of yourself into old
unfolding into new
where you will find your power.

-your new voice

a Woman
of Colour
encased in skin the lighter side of honey,
crowned in waves,
with features that confuse
but do not
immediately
bring to surface
the hate and fear of Other(s).

a Muslim
who does not
wear hijab on her skin
but in her heart.

an Other
who has never
lived the discrimination daily experienced
by her darker skinned sisters
or those who wear a halo of fabric
or those who break English inside their mouths.

a Sister
who recognizes her privilege exists
because she is breathing
the poison of a sick world.

-'what do you see when you look in the mirror'

today is a day
when i have to tie my hands beneath my rib cage.

because today
if i do not bind these hands
i am terrified that i will reach through my softness
to everyone
who has been quiet. complicit. loud. implicit
everyone.
everyone.
every. one,
and squeeze their life from their hearts.

-Al Nakba | 15 may (1948)

i was born
by the salt-waters
of the Mediterranean,
covered in grains of golden sand dust.

today's popular narrative
sells
that -

she has never fallen into beauty,
is at present without it,
will never find her way to magnificence.

that
the way of the civilized
is inside of clean lines and perfect beginnings
without pain. error. mess,
revolution.

that
the way of the civilized
is in light(er) skin. small(er) & (more) efficient features,
surrounded by straight(er) hair, highlights of feather.

that
the way of the civilized
is british, and then american-accented
with emotions held at bay,
locked behind closed doors
because what is an emotion
but a confession to an unsolved problem,
& the civilized
they have no problems

[and so,
(too) logically then,
no emotion?]

that
i would
choke
on those grains of golden sand dust
drown
in that salt-water.

-the lies i continue to unlearn

a Principal
who built schools across an Occupied land,
after raising generations to their full height
he retired to his bookstore
filled with heartbreak. heroism. poetry. politics. theology,
all knowledge,

the covers i liquefied
the pages into which i burrowed
emerging into new minds,

and out of which he often carried me
asleep
with hands fisted around paper
held to my small chest
helping my heart beat.

-how i learned to speak

from a young age
i learned
to eat lemon
dipped in salt.

this. a ritual
turned later
to metaphor.

-in sourness is treasure

live simply.
help generously.

-distilled, articles of my Faith

once more
i am seeking forgiveness.

cautiously
i come to my knees
place my palms across her belly
ask if she will let me stay.
(my absences can be so long.)

she is quiet
but her gentle fragrance kisses
and i have her answer.

i lay myself at her feet.
her waves take me home.

-Islam

my Prophet
he taught
that you cannot see into hearts
like He can see into hearts
and so: we are all One.

Unified
of Him. in Him.
Whole together.

how can you continue
to believe that your paler skin
elevates you in station
when we will all
to Him return.

-a question to my Ummah | we need to talk about your hate

drowning in grief,
suffocating on bereavement,
i often envy the dead.

because this place is not a just one
it was not intended to be a fair one
rather a trial
to choose good or otherwise
and at His gate, walk through the door of our choosing –

freedom of will washing this back
and entry to Truth.

when broken against mo(u)rning,
exhausted by this world
sand-paper against my heart
i am often piqued
by the place where there is quenching Light
certainly gentler than the here.

-and to Him when i return | a Muslim lullaby

my hands
unlearned
would reach for him
hoping to pull loose
a thread of love.

they were always too small
my reach too short.

-my father's sweater

she would orchestrate feasts for 30,
the only way to keep him home.

i would watch her
water flour for him
swell it with yeast to fill each room
the size of her love and want and confusion
conversations kneaded he would not have,
a rose-water prayer that
27 people would speak her bread
into his heart-awareness.

-the baker | before the divorce

at dinner
they argued about this. that. this and that.

i turned my eyes
curved into my plate
begged the flowers come to life
willing them to catch small and quiet teardrops
to swell a space into their gold-rimmed garden
of china
large enough
to welcome (away) my small self.

-a child and her plate

she has her father's hands
filled with soft oceans.

to sleep
i would lay next to him
listening to The Voice of Peace
salt-water air filling the room
as i wrapped my small hands around his
(my body a fraction of an already small bed)
dreaming new worlds
safe worlds
beyond Occupation
which is where he is now.

today
when i take her hands in mine
i feel their soft oceans.

i do not know. i do not know.
idonotknow
what will happen to me
when she takes her oceans to meet her father's
and leaves me ashore.

-grief | mother | ummi

the women
matrilineal of my ancestors
we dream to life.

my mother's most important dream,
that she sat with Muhammad
a light on her face.

this will be the glue
keeping me together
when she leaves to be Kept in Peace.

-a reminder to myself when the time comes

she lays one hand
across my forehead
recites Quran
the other she cups
catches my sadness
drinks
cool-breezes into this scorched heart.

the ocean is inside her.

-Sumaya. whose name means Of Heaven

you ask me:
fawn,
split in two,
why do you
expose
the soft new glow of your pelt
to only those from whom
you know
you must guard it
so violently.

because –
i don't remember
my father leaving

only that
he stopped arriving

and this

this *stopped arriving*
i had to unlearn
that this is what
i should expect from men.

because –
i watched his mouth from which
burning words fell and charred black
raw and wet
her once honey skin
and i want love
(i, want love?)

but am still learning
that this
it is not
love.

-daughter of divorce | history of a commitment phobe

i was ruptured from my father
broken into small fragments
scattered.
lost to myself,
a diaspora within a diaspora.

i learned
that he too had been splintered
when -

pilgrim,
he came searching
carrying a bag of silk
edged in gold
opened with a richness of apology.

he gathered within it all of my pieces
spoke fire into each
and welded me whole.

-bond

sat across from me
he took his heart from his rib cage
placed it beneath my knife.
his tongue from his mouth
laid it tip to my pen.

i imagined cutting myself from his chest
writing pain into his speech.

instead
his tears came from my eyes
flooding my heart
resuscitating my life
that i did not know had been lost.

-healing | father | abbi

i wear his wedding band on my thumb
touch it to my heart when i am blind
wait for his hand to find mine
lead me to safety.

-Monzer. whose name means He Who Warns of Danger

his name
would sit comfortably
in the part of her mouth where she is most at peace.

the language
which she believed
would provide refuge for her daughter.

but.
because the language knows
the precise syntax. exact grammar
of me. in me
since birth,

his name
was the one that reformed me
to greatest injury.

-my mother(‘s) tongue

one hand
money-covered fingers stretch
for the just-formed hips
of little girls.

the other
jerking policy. culture. religion
to regulate the salt-waters of women
hips swelled with the weight of life.

-(some) tools of oppression belong to the same body

it is used as a dirty word
when the alternative is to be called simple,
expecting instead sugar and spice. everything nice.

it strips us of our right to be challenging. explosive. difficult.

worse, it denies
women
their fullness,
a throw-away word
used
to describe us
who refuse to be pliable.

-'complicated'

‘the same men will be attracted to you and to her
but for different reasons…’

articulating
what he thought would warm me
spread my legs (as it had others) –

some imagined distinction between the woman
inside of whose belly men rest their ego
and the woman from whose belly they siphon for pleasure.

i softened my mouth to welcome his
feeling for that split tongue
bit down and bled him
until all of the women on whom this had worked
drained from his body into mine
and woke to remember themselves
while he to nothing.

-on the love affair between male misogyny and female
misogyny

in her village

there is a hearth
anchored deep
around which
each home
is forever built.

the sisters,
eating self-hate
birth
a spark of rage
lighting this hearth
in which they lay
a mo(u)ld
for a needle.

cherries,
are these mo(u)lds picked
from passages within Faith.

the brothers,
vomiting ego
prick
knees
to flow the tonic
of unblemished blood
into the mo(u)ld.

the village
with heart turned away from Him,
confidence from self,
collects the needles

to sew her honour.

-hym(e)n

do not lie to other women
or pit yourself against other women.
do not speak poorly of them
or elevate yourself at their cost.
do not hurt them
or disgrace them
or disrespect other women.

every time you do
you cut yourself
and We have bled out for long enough.

-The (only) Rules

suddenly a stranger,
i watched – film real –
as he murdered the smile on her mouth
soundtrack, of decomposition.

quietly, i thought: men do not do harm
is what it should be
but is not.

her eyes (s)wept
the room
caught mine, cast their net
inside of which i placed myself
peacefully
knowing that i would soon be
the sustenance
of her blood-let heart.

-on the bond that is female friendship

pronounced *taslyah* -

the Arabic word for (meaningless) pastime
undertaken only for the pleasure
of the doer
when bored.

like the cracking of sunflower seeds,
a half of which are chewed up just to be spit out.

you
you are not a *taslyah.*

you are permitted to refuse.

you are allowed to say: no.
you are authorized to say: this is not enough.

because
your values
they are to be found: in sacred stations.

you are empowered to decline
scraps. handouts. bullshit. rubbish
from anyone. everyone. who sees you ever. in any way.
as an object
for consumption
in their exercise of gluttony.

you are not permitted
to be less.

-a love letter | sanctioned to value

i was listening to Allah run his warm winds

across my fabric walls,
eyes
on silken floors pulling these feet when -

my mouth, wet with honey, tripped
and was caught gently
landing on his lips
rose-water filled, cinnamon-dusted
then simmered
on open fires,

(you,
like hand-written letters
swelled by humidity
at the tip of fingers stained by honey & palm trees.)

we fell
toes touching night skies
poured into velvet sands,
my body between his hands.

-love oasis

i walked into his open mouth
searching for the right sentence
found the end of its thread
pulled it out after me –

outside,
focused,
i passed it through an eye
and wove it into wool
to calm my heart.

-security blanket

his lashes dusted my skin in cinnamon
as he lowered his brow
slid his eyes down my neck
and found the scar-covered spot against which
my trembling
hands were pressing their palms.

gently coaxing them away
nearing his mouth
keeping his eyes focused (on himself)
he sang me a song
with lips sealed.

i heard
so stepped from the ledge.

-how i learned that i could not fly

i undress
fold and place my skin on his chair
stand still
wait for his direction
wondering how will he get this blood out of his afghan.

‘i like you. i don’t want to hurt you.’

said with ease. and liquor. and other things. chemical things.
it rolled over his tongue
split itself across that wet mouth
dripped
caught by my thirsty heart
leaving
greasy film -

‘don’t worry. there is nothing left to cut.’

-the lies we told one another

there is a space created
cavernous
after the shattering of security
a no(wo)man's land.

i watched,
her movements slow
as she crept along its floor
to scrounge the scraps
(with intention)
he had left.

she picked them up
carefully,
making love to each,
pushing them through
every incision
he had manipulated
on to her body.

horror,
i think,
how neatly her skin closes behind
his garbage
rising green
across her once beautiful skin.

-the abusive relationship

i could not kill it
so
first i placed my fingers at my tongue
then quietly reached past my throat
found its beginning
and pulled
believing i could remove it instead –

i pulled.

i pulled
and unwound my feet.
i pulled
and amputated my legs.
i pulled
and uncoiled my belly. ribs
laying flat
- i kept pulling
because i could not kill it –

i pulled.

i pulled
and up came my
breasts
then my hands
which caught in my throat
so i could not pull it anymore.

eyes on the ceiling
my care for you
a thick rope of my body
between my lips. alive against my tongue
my care for you
still present

and most of me undone.

-emotion dysmorphic disorder

be mindful
to whom
you give a building permit.

-emotional real-estate

you entered on my condition that
you leave your heart outside my latched door.

and when you came in,
i ripped away your fingernails
declawed your tongue
burnt your eyes
blunted your hair
because you
simply
could not
be important enough.
to inflict pain.

-the only way i would know you

i spilled tea
burning the counter
while trying to speak.

you would not have a conversation
because
truth is the only thing which lives in my mouth.

this,
a sign that
the spilled tea
was not in error.

-intuition

i refused the creation of borders
believed the earth's surface
limitless filled
all and infinite possibility,
mountain-range solitude
salt-kisses of ocean
forested lushness,
each held in our bodies. affection. care
the only passports required.

how was i to know
you are a Patriot.

-me, the global citizen

thumb and forefinger reached to the right of my collarbone
he conjured a zipper and pulled across to my left shoulder
then downwards
slow. smooth
until the ribs
a small snag which he works through carefully
without any tears or broken teeth
slow. smooth again
at my hip he turns and heads right once more
stops
pulls the sheet of skin away
touches my organs.
(fingers sticky leave residue
i think he even cut something across his ragged nails.)

he is gone
and i won't blink
so i don't lose sight
of the zipper
i fumble.

yes. definitely.
he cut something across his ragged nails.

-fingerprints

watch out
for men
with teeth
in their eyes.

-(fore)warning(s)

(i thought i saw the devils
beneath the waves,
turned my face
asked Him for clarity.)

i was walking the shoreline with care
quietly when
Faith as his boat
he came to my shore
took my hand and asked
to build.

fearful. hesitant.
i did not know if his boat
would keep.

knees bent beneath me
brow dusted prayer,
i accepted and built beautiful.
i built beautiful.
following his arc, i built.

paused
and looked for his boat
but found only water
as it sank my legs
took with it
our sand-castle.

he is leaving
water in his mouth
nose apart, body swelling
bruised blue
so many devils
chains all over his feet

pulling him beneath.

free, where the devil's hands
can never touch me
i am walking ashore
us washing my back
alone.

(i see the devils
beneath the waves,
returned my heart
to Him to keep.)

-shoreline of an addict

underlined by the heat of fire
they were two stars
glittering –

pulling my body to a destination
unidentified
some(any)where
surely, a promise of safety.

sea storm in my eyes,
its river heavy
downhill flowing
pushing itself into my mouth
the only water i drank for weeks
to soften the drought.

this heart displaced,
her feet lead sinking into
my new status
forced across a map born of the violence
and war between us.

-refugee

three to our walks
you. me. the day-break's humid blanket
which
today
i wrap as shawl
to warm against the cold
of walks
without you.

-leftovers

‘your life. heart. head lines
have been ripped and reoriented.
why?’

‘he left
without the kindness of conversation.
the empty static
meant that i had to dig for answers.
this excavation
left wedges and splinters of him in my hands
each a question i cannot answer.

can you help me
please?’

-conversation with a palm reader

she could not help herself.
it's not that she wanted to cook a bad meal
it's that she could not give softness away
outside of her skin
and so cooked, though in earnest,
nauseating food.

she could not help herself.
it's not that she wanted the stains to deepen
it's that she could not give kindness away
outside of her skin
and so cleaning, though in earnest,
encouraged the filth.

she could not help herself.

it's not that she didn't want to love and be kind,
it is that
she had been flayed and broken
hung upside down and drained
that she could not help herself but
to turn the tap inward
in order to keep what little was left
inside of her skin
replenish and drown in her first love,
(remembering) self-love,
before she could once more
offer water
at the lips of another.

-my secrets, spoken in the third person

it is not
your responsibility
to ice the fists
which beat you.

-self-care

i point at my wrist and ask
'would you please do it here.
this is where i heal.
thank you.'

his eyes are shaded
precision is perfect.
diamond scalpel in hand
he slides it softly in
to flay (un)virgin skin.

another man
steps into the shadows of my history.

i dip the nib into my vein
breathe
scratch the nib across the clean white surface
trap my truth on paper
sit back
heal.

healed
i turn my eyes toward the next.

with finger at my wrist i ask
'would you please do it here.
this is where i heal.
thank you.'

-masochist

i water vulnerability into them
dripping from my heart
where i am safely swimming.

i feed hope into them
falling drops from my eyes
where i am most honestly living.

and when they die –
because this is what flowers do –
at their fullest, swollen by my care,

i am not broken by the sadness
but swelled with shine
that they lived to their fullest intention
and have seeded
unseen
the genesis of future blossoms.

-horticulturalist

that your softness cannot be depleted,

that all hearts are soft and full,

that the empty hearts can be filled,

and so when you give and give and give
there will come a day when you might stop.

-the lies we are taught | on loving a narcissist

the heart-pain i feel
is in direct proportion
to your ability to love
i reminded myself.

to envy the quick shedding of a lover
is to turn your back
on the softest you.

-self-awareness

i look at you, curious –

sliced between blades
under pressure
you become
more intentioned
performing
as your creator bid
blessed,
in meeting your purpose
always,
leaving your mark.

whereas i.
i will search
for my meaning
who am I?
until we fall
into
this same earth.

-pencil | is ‘to love’ a purpose, i wonder

i am trying to forgive you.

but to forgive. means to let go. and the letting go. is another denouement. and the new beginning. requires a page break. and the fresh page. demands a new paragraph. and the first letter. requests a dropped capital. best articulated in a new font.

because it is this new font
that is the genesis
and the re-imagining
of potential and unknown others
inside of an already thick tome
of existing compositions.

and i.
i am tired.
of writing.

-scribe

that we
fall
in love
is an untruth.

there is only
ascension.

-rise

we are born
safely held
(ingredients).

at the hands of others
their love soft. manipulation hard,
we are simmered by the pain.

changed
by the simmering.
grateful
for the simmering.
parenthesis evaporated.

in my grandmother's recipe book –

rose-water syrup:
lemon, sugar, rose-water.
combine.
simmer.

-elemental | rebirth

Acknowledgments

In late 2016, I refused to let pain be the only thing which he left at my feet. From that, all but two poems in the lover section were written through early 2017.

All pieces in all other sections were born from this same voice, inshAllah evolved voice, over the last two years, though rooted in far different experiences and perspectives.

I wish to thank all of my beloved family and friends for supporting my work through all of its phases - the good, the bad, and the ugly. Most especially, I would like to thank all of the safe spaces created by these same beloveds, in their efforts to nurture this voice, and to calm this heart's tumult.

Special thanks to Tyseer Aboulnasr for being the first to turn one of my pieces into a printed book. To Aalya Ahmed for forcing me to finally, in 2012, put forth my writing in my real name. To Chimene Suleyman, a woman whose work I revere, for always being so supportive of my work. To Azza Abbaro for helping me choose the pieces between your hands, and for making my vision of rose-water syrup*'s cover page a reality. To Jennifer Morgan Jones for the beautiful art work serving as back-drop to my photograph. To Cyberwit for believing in me at a time when I did not believe in myself. And to my aunts Nuha and Amal, and cousins Reem and Deema for always serving as safest landings for this heart.*

Lastly, to my parents. I am nothing without you; may my actions only ever bring you lightness and love. Please stay a while.

www.ingramcontent.com/pod-product-compliance
Lightning Source LLC
Chambersburg PA
CBHW050023170726
48282CB00025B/525
* 9 7 8 9 3 8 9 0 7 4 1 5 4 *